Also by Elizabeth N. Doyd

**The Love Book:** Writing Your Way to Your Soul Mate

**Write Him Off:** 30 Days to Heal Your Broken Heart

**Gratitude Journal:** 52 Writing Prompts to Celebrate Your Wonderful Life

**The Science of Getting Rich Action Plan:** Decoding Wallace D. Wattles's Bestselling Book

# 7 Days to Minimalist Living

*A Stress-Free Guide to Declutter, Clean & Organize Your Home & Your Life*

Elizabeth N. Doyd

Copyright © 2014 by Elizabeth N. Doyd

All rights reserved.

No part of this publication may be reproduced, distributed or transmitted in any form or by any means, including photocopying, recording, or any other electronic or mechanical methods, without the prior written permission of the publisher, except in the case of brief quotations embodied in critical reviews and certain other noncommercial uses permitted by copyright law.

In practical advice books, like anything else in life, there are no guarantees of results. This book is not intended for use as a source of medical advice. All readers are advised to seek services of competent professionals in the medical field as needed.

ISBN-13: 978-1987859058

ISBN-10: 1987859057

# Contents

| | |
|---|---|
| Introduction | 7 |
| How to Use this Book | 13 |
| | |
| LIGHTEN UP: Understanding Clutter | 15 |
| Why You Hold On To Things | 17 |
| Why You Need to Declutter and What You Really Value | 21 |
| What You Really Value | 23 |
| How to Recognize Clutter | 25 |
| Things to Toss Immediately | 27 |
| | |
| MAKE A PLAN | 29 |
| Your 7 Day Plan | 31 |
| Tips on Decluttering and Organizing | 34 |
| Selling Your Things | 37 |
| | |
| DECLUTTER, CLEAN & ORGANIZE | 39 |
| Entryway | 41 |
| Kitchen/Minimalist Cooking | 43 |
| What to Avoid | 46 |
| Decluttering Tips | 49 |
| Living Room | 52 |
| Bathroom | 53 |
| Bedroom | 55 |
| Children's Rooms & Their Things | 57 |
| Teenager Bedrooms | 60 |
| Garage, Basement, Garden | 62 |
| Office | 64 |
| Computer & Internet | 67 |
| Technology | 72 |
| Closets | 73 |
| Minimalist Wardrobe | 77 |
| Minimalist Car | 81 |
| Mail | 83 |
| Collections | 85 |

| | |
|---|---:|
| Sentimental Objects and Gifts | 87 |
| Photos | 88 |
| Cards & Letters | 90 |
| Music | 91 |
| Digital Decluttering | 92 |
| People | 93 |
| Other People's Clutter | 98 |
| Minimalist Checklist | 99 |
| Maintain Your Space | 99 |
| Conclusion | 101 |
| About the Author | 103 |

# Introduction

When you're at home, do you feel anxious, overwhelmed and sometimes even depressed, but don't know why?

Your first clue is to look at your surroundings. Clutter can overwhelm your senses, even unconsciously. The mess in your home is often a reflection of your inner state.

When you have inner clutter, it expands to your environment. This can show up as disorganization, junk, and hoarding. By uncovering your clutter, buried emotions can come to the surface.

Is your house teeming with stuff? Particularly stuff you don't need or like all that much? Basement, bedrooms, closets, cabinets—every nook and cranny overflowing with stuff you hardly touch.

The extraneous things we own weigh us down. The overstuffed drawers, the lack of counter space, the junk shoved under beds—they consume space and drain energy from our surroundings. The stacks of papers and files on your desk, the books you'll never read, the clothes you don't wear are all dead weight in what could be your sanctuary after a long hard day at work.

Now imagine walking into your home and seeing only your favorite things. You cherish each piece of furniture and can't wait to relax in your favorite chair. All the clothes in your closet are pieces you want to wear. The music in your collection are only the songs you want to listen to. Everything is clean and in their place. All the things you own only add value to your life. When you're home, you feel peaceful and light. Everything you want is easily found. Home finally equates to comfort.

This book will help you get there. You might find that throwing out even a couple of garbage bags can feel better than therapy. You'll lose that claustrophobic feeling and breathe again. I'll show you how to clear the clutter from your life to focus on what's truly important. Chances are, 75% of the things in your home are no benefit to your life at all.

Possessions are like anchors. They tie you down, yet you're afraid of losing them. When you let them go, you also let go of greed, obsession and overworking.

Don't let the word minimalism scare you. It's not about getting rid of modern advancements and living in the stone age. It's about keeping things that are useful, meaningful and add value to your life.

While it does not place importance on materials things and money at the expense of health, relationships, passions, growth, and communications, contribution, minimalism is also not about denying yourself of the things you need.

Minimalism is clearing the clutter from your life to focus on what's truly important. You'll have no distractions when you live a minimalist lifestyle. You're making room for the things you do want to come into your life.

The less stuff you have, the less time, energy and space it takes to maintain it. It frees up your own time, energy and space to let in more love and happiness.

Here some more benefits:

- You will need less and do more.
- More time on your hands. No more searching for things. No more moving a million boxes when you change residences, less time needed to clean and maintain.
- More focus on what gives our lives meaning, joy and value.
- Find your passions.

- By clearing away the noise, we can concentrate on peace and spirituality in a meditative space.
- Lower stress.
- Lessens cost and debt.
- More time to get healthy and active.
- More sustainable living.
- Living in the moment.
- Experience lasting joys over temporary hits of happiness.

You don't need to be a vegan or a monk to be a minimalist. While eating healthy, going green, and living a peaceful life is consistent with minimalism, it's adaptable to fit in with your usual routine.

Minimalism is also not about being frugal. Is it really better to buy cheap items that will break down sooner rather than invest in something that will last a lifetime? Minimalism is about long-term fulfillment. It's about quality over quantity. It's about value.

What one person values is different from what another person values. Everyone must find their own path, which is why the "Make the Plan" section of the book guides you on how to form your own action plan.

The stuff we don't value are merely filling a void. When we go shopping as sport or recreation, we are merely trying to fill this void. Our consumeristic society only makes it worse, bombarding us with ads that use fear tactics to try to convince us that we need their product or our world will fall apart. They make it difficult for us to distinguish whether the product is something we genuinely want. When you declutter, you'll clear out all those false promises and reveal what really matters.

If you have trouble letting go, don't worry. This book is full of practical advice and essential tools for you to live the life you've always wanted.

Are you avoiding positive change by hanging on to things? Physical things won't miss you. Living with less is the first step to a peaceful mind. It makes space for the new to come in.

Happiness naturally arrives when you are surrounded by things and people that you genuinely want in your life. You'll be more efficient and focused on your priorities.

You'll also be able to heal. When you clean up the skeletons in your closets, you'll feel much lighter, emotionally and physically. Stop making excuses. Don't let the things you own end up owning you. Take your life back. Let's get started.

*— Elizabeth N. Doyd*

# How to Use this Book

If you want to clean and declutter a certain room right away, feel free to go to skip to the appropriate chapter to find the specific advice you need. If you want to do a deep cleanse of your whole place however, grab a pen and a notebook.

Use a plain notebook just for this purpose. As you may know from my other books, I'm a fan of journaling and writing things down. When you formulate a plan with a to-do list, especially one with deadlines, you'll be more motivated to tackle the challenges.

You don't need to start an extensive journal for this project—a simple plan is enough. What better way to get organized than having an organized plan? This is especially useful if you live in a big home or have a lot of stuff.

It's funny how we often identify with our stuff as if they are a part of us. But you are not your things. If something gets stolen, you're not going to bleed. That car, that designer purse, the iPod or the smartphone is not an extension of yourself.

Elizabeth N. Doyd

# LIGHTEN UP
## Understanding Clutter

# Why You Hold On To Things

There are many reasons why we can't seem to let certain things go, even if they are not serving us in any practical way.

### Security

A main reason is security. We hold onto material things to feel more secure, but the paradox is that by clinging to these things, it drains our energy and leaves us feeling frustrated and overwhelmed. When we keep things to guard against our fear of loss, we'll keep looking for more things to make us feel more secure until we have an entire house full of stuff we don't need or use.

Security is the reason we stay in bad relationships, out of fear of being alone, for example. But if we let go of what is not serving us, we make room for the amazing relationship that we really deserve. This is also the case with material things.

### Addiction

When we buy something, we associate that thing with a feeling. We make the mistake of thinking that this thing is the key to our joy because it's exciting or it gives us comfort, but the thing itself does not have life. Sure, buying something cool gives you a high, but the buzz doesn't last. It's like a sugar high; it'll make you empty in the long run if you depend on it to give you long-term fulfillment. When the novelty wears off, you'll look around for your next fix, and the first item simply hangs around at home, serving no purpose. It's an addiction: you bought it because it made you feel good, but when the inert object only takes up space in your life, it's controlling you.

### Approval

Humans have an inherent need to be liked. We like to show off, and one of the ways we do it is with the material representations of what we think we're about. It's why we keep a library full of books we'll never read to show that we're intelligent, or prominently showcase all our ribbons and trophies, or buy the latest iPhone, handbags and cars.

### Identity

We may even identify with our things. Some people distinguish themselves with their profession and how much money they make. Others do it with the clothes they wear, the music they listen to, or the objects they collect. That's why they get upset when something is stolen or broken.

### Automatic Collections

Sometimes collections form because we subscribe to magazines and catalogs, or receive handwritten cards and letters. Perhaps well-meaning friends and family heard that you collect angel figurines and now it's all you ever get on birthdays and holidays. This can be a hard addiction to break because we've invested some time and energy into maintaining this collection, plus others have also come to identify our collection with us as well.

### The "Someday" Pile

Many of us like to keep books, letters, self-help tapes, articles and other things around because we tell ourselves that we'll get to it when we have time. Months or years later, they're still sitting around untouched. You have to ask yourself if these are things you really want to do, or if they are things you feel you should do in order to be the person you think you're supposed to be, or who other people expect you to be. It could be out of feelings of inadequacy, that you're not quite complete until you learn this or do that.

### Holding On To The Past

Sometimes it's hard to let go of things because they remind us of the joys we've had in life. But the things do not hold the joy itself, but rather the memories of joy. It may also hold the unfulfilled expectations that you're still waiting to receive from it. We hold on because we may be afraid that the same joy will not come again. It keeps us stuck because it's also a fear of change. If we hold on to the same things, our life remains the same, and it keeps us from moving forward.

### Obligations To Others

Sometimes we simply want to please others and make them happy. When we're given presents we don't like, we still feel the need to keep or display it. Sometimes this gets out of hand and we're burdened with a whole house of inherited things—furniture, clothing, etc.—and we secretly turn resentful.

Read on, as this book will give you advice on how to speak up for yourself and let go of things you don't really want.

## Why You Need to Declutter and Find What You Really Value

By becoming aware of why you are attached to your things, you can **let go of old beliefs** in an instant. When you simplify your life, you simplify your mind and inner being. By opening your physical and emotional space, you'll also **open yourself up to new opportunities**.

Sometimes a collection of things is like a time capsule or mausoleum—it buries you in the past. Clearing your surroundings allows you to **see your home, your life, and yourself for what they really are**. Sometimes people refuse to get rid of the clutter because they are afraid of change.

Having too many things competing for your attention can also be overwhelming. It can cause stress and anxiety. **A minimalistic space allows you to breathe**. You'll have more time if you are organized. You can save up to an hour each day if you're not constantly searching for things you've misplaced.

People can also be clutter. Do you have a toxic partner or friend? You might've been holding on to them because, like with things, you're familiar with them and they provide a level of comfort. At one point they were important to you, but as you mature, you may now find that they no longer suit you or your life. By letting them go, you free up your life and theirs. Love is supposed to be freeing. You'll be able to **open yourself to new people** and allow yourself the space to cultivate meaningful relationships.

**When you need less, you can do more.** You'll be able to grow into your best self when you surround yourself with only the things and values that benefit you.

In a calm environment, you'll have the meditative space to **be more in tune with yourself**. Instead of turning to material things for security, you'll learn that real security comes from within: deep down we know what gives us value, which relationships are healthy, and what we want to do with our time.

When you **stop shopping as a form of therapy**, you **stop wasting money**. The excitement that we get when we see something shiny at the mall wears off quickly, sometimes as soon as we get home. We may temporarily bask in the light of the object's potential, but when it doesn't fulfill our needs, it gathers dust as we look for next thing.

# What You Really Value

To break the cycle, you must get rid of the things you no longer need. First, ask yourself what you really value.

**Exercise #1:**

Make a list of the top 10 things you own from the most expensive to the least expensive.

Now make a second list of the top 10 things that makes you happy.

Is there an overlap between the two at all?

**Exercise #2:**

At the end of your life, what do you want people to remember you for? Pick 3 things. Is it your qualities or the things that you own?

If you're having a hard time with this, write down 3 great qualities of someone you admire.

Stuff can help you reach your goals, but your goals shouldn't be to obtain more stuff. It's fulfillment that you're after—love, friendship, sharing, adventure, laughter...

## How to Recognize Clutter

You're hurting no one's feelings when you toss your junk out. This doesn't mean you have to throw out everything you own and sit in a white room in order to live a minimalist lifestyle. Go with your gut and keep only what makes you happy.

Society tends to send the message that owning things in general, lots and lots of things, is valuable. Sometimes the mind wants to trick us into believing that many of the things we own do make us happy when they are really clutter. It can be difficult to recognize. Even when your home is well-organized, clutter is still clutter: all the organizers that you bought to contain your unwanted stuff are really expensive trash cans.

It's easy to recognize the things you love. Your gut can usually tell you which things you actually want to keep. However, sometimes it can be a challenge to recognize what is really serving us or not.

For example, my son had an electric guitar and amp set up in his bedroom for years. We had spent good money on it. He started playing when he was fourteen, but he lost interest in it after a couple of years. The guitar set would have given incredible value to someone else, but for my son, it became a burden when his desire to play music was gone. It took up space in his room, and every time he looked at it, he would feel guilt for not playing the guitar and for wasting the money we spent on it. Every once in a while, he'd pick it up and try to reignite the passion, but it never lasted.

Finally, we all agreed that the guitar had to go. Nobody was getting any value from it in our home. In fact, it made my son resentful towards it. He sold the set to someone who was thrilled to buy a guitar and amp in such good condition for a low price.

So just because you once loved something, it doesn't mean you need to hold on to it for life. Move the old relics and corpses out with no guilt. If the desire is not there anymore, you're crushing nobody's dreams.

# Things to Toss Immediately

**Broken things.** Why keep them around? Broken things cause disharmony in the energy of your home. If you love the thing and really want to fix it, put it in a cardboard box designated for things to repair, and do so as soon as you can.

**Things you don't like.** Did you only keep it around because it was expensive or because it was a gift? If you don't like it, you're doing nobody any favors by keeping it.

**Old newspapers, magazines and catalogs.** Why keep yesterday's news around? If you ever need an old article, they are archived.

**Outdated technology.** Beepers and fax machines aren't coming back any time soon.

**Things you haven't used for more than 6 months.** If you're not getting use or value out of it, it's gone.

IF YOU'RE UNSURE, ASK YOURSELF:

**When was the last time I used this?**

**Do I want this?**

**Do I like this?**

**Do I need this?**

**Can I let it go?**

**Am I keeping this for me or to impress others?**

**Does this make me happy?**

**What would happen if I got rid of this?**

**Can someone else use this more than me?**

If you find yourself over-debating to keep something, it's clutter. Happiness is simple. When something brings us joy, we know it right away.

If you are really having a hard time letting some things go, ask a friend over for a second opinion. You can try to "sell" your friends the item in question as an exercise. You'll know by your sales pitch whether the item is worth keeping or not, and so will your friend.

Elizabeth N. Doyd

# MAKE A PLAN

# Your 7 Day Plan

Take your notebook and pen. Pretend to be a real estate agent or a perspective buyer of your home as you walk around. Be conscious and sensitive to every room and everything in each room.

Which rooms make you feel the most uncomfortable? Are there objects screaming for attention? What areas would require more time to tackle?

Note your observations down.

Make a list of all the rooms in your home: *kitchen, living room, main bedroom, kid's bedroom, bathroom 1, bathroom 2, guest room, garage*, etc.

Rate each room from 1 to 5, 1 being the room that needs the least decluttering, cleaning and organizing, and 5 being the room that needs drastic attention. List the rooms from the highest priority to lowest.

You may live in a big house that requires a lot of attention, or a tiny studio apartment. By dividing the decluttering process into a manageable plan, you'll be more likely to stick with it.

7 days is long enough to tackle even the largest spaces, and short enough not to make this process feel like a full-time job. If you have a busy work week, you can do this on the weekends if each room requires a full day to tackle. Or if you think you'll only need a couple of hours each day to dedicate to your tasks, carve out the time after work to do so. Just be clear on what you are doing each day, and stick with it.

Be realistic about how much time you'll need to declutter, clean and organize each room. If the living room is in the worst shape out of the rest of the house and it really requires a full day, do so. Get the worst room in the best shape first and the rest will follow.

If you live with your family, explain to them what you're doing. Tell them all the benefits they'll receive from having a clean home, and include them in the plan. If you have kids, give them assignments and get them excited about helping. If they are young and need your supervision, carve out a day or two (depending on how many kids you have) and supervise them as they sort through their clutter. Explain to them that cleaning the home is important, the way we need to bathe to keep our bodies clean.

When you're sorting with them, ask them to tell you what they think about each item, whether to keep or toss. Follow what they say. At the end of each cleaning day, give them a reward. This gives the kids a sense of responsibility and pride, as well as a voice in family decision-making. To get them to donate more, you can hold a contest. For example, whoever donates the most toys wins a prize.

If you have grown children and they are not on board with the plan, don't force them. Clean your space and see if they follow suit. Focus on your own life and give them the freedom to be inspired by you. Don't take away that choice by forcing your new values on them, or cleaning their rooms for them. They are the ones who must live in that room.

## Tips on Decluttering and Organizing

Prepare empty boxes or labelled trash bags for:
- Things to toss
- Things to donate to charity
- Things to repair
- Things to sell

You may also prepare boxes/bags for
- Things to relocate into another room
- Things that belong to someone else who doesn't live there anymore
- Things you want to give away to people you know

At the end of each day, take out the trash. For the donation items, or things to give/return to other people, put the boxes/bags into your car if you drive or by the front door, so that you'll be reminded to give them away as soon as possible. Sort the "relocation items" in their proper locations.

Set goals for each day. Carve out a time during the day to do this when you are clear-headed, which is when you can make the best decisions. If you're a morning person, do it then. You'll be more effective this way.

*Remember:*

- If you don't use it, lose it!
- Place like with like.
- It's okay to toss out furniture and big items!
- If it's expensive, you can always sell it.
- Store frequently used items where you can use them because you'll be more likely to store them back when you're done.
- Make sure the things you use on a regular basis is accessible.
- Assign homes for everything.
- Color-coded labelling helps.

- Storage with lids keeps the dust off stuff.
- Lean how to say no. Only allow the right things into your life: the things you want, like, and have a passion for.

## Selling Your Things

If you have a lot of things to sell, hold a garage sale. You can even ask your neighbors, family, or friends if they'd like to participate. Make the sale on a weekend, barring holiday weekends when people are out of town. Create colorful signs to put up around your neighborhood and place ads in the community newspaper or online classified ads.

Organize and price all of your merchandise before the sale. Do slash prices at the end of the sale. The goal is to get rid of everything! Donate the unsold items to charity.

You can also sell things online on Ebay and Amazon. If you would rather not deal with the hassle of sending items by post, or have things that are too large or costly to ship, such as furniture, you can try Craigslist.org, kijiji.com, gumtree.com, or other online classified ads. Post clear pictures and describe the condition of the item truthfully.

Since potential buyers are strangers, be cautious. Don't allow them into your home. Arrange to meet in a public place during the day, preferably with a friend. If they must come to your home to pick up a heavy item, it's best to have your item outside the door ready for them to take away. Make sure that you have a friend or two with you so you're not alone.

There are also other ways to sell your goods. You can book a booth at a community center sale or at a local flea market. Used bookstores will also buy your old books, movies and music. Consignment stores will sell your clothes and accessories and take a percentage of the sale.

Elizabeth N. Doyd

# DECLUTTER, CLEAN & ORGANIZE

# Entryway

Entryways can get messy since it's the place where you come in and drop things off. A **coat rack** or a set of **hooks** will organize all the jackets and coats from your family or guests. If it rains a lot where you live, an **umbrella holder** will keep your umbrellas handy.

A **pretty bowl** can hold the small things that people forget before they go out, such as keys or wallets.

If people in your family are constantly misplacing their keys, a wall-mounted key-holder with the name of each person under each key hook will allow them to hang their keys when they come in, and remind them to take them when they go out. You'll also be able to see who is in or out of the house with a quick glance.

Designate a place for new mail coming in so they don't get tossed from table to table and possibly get lost and forgotten. It's ideal to open your mail right away and deal with what you can on hand, whether that's tossing away the junk, or filing the bills in a "To Pay" folder in your office. However, life can get hectic and you might not have the right frame of mind to sort through new mail as soon as you get home. You can use a wall-mounted **mail holder** or one that sits on your entryway table to keep them organized for when you are ready to read them.

Shoes can pile up pretty fast if you let them. Keep the out of season shoes (such as snow boots in the summer) somewhere else, as well as shoes you only wear on occasion, such as high heels or dress shoes for special evenings. A **shoe rack** will save floor space and keep your house slippers separate from your outdoor shoes.

When it's winter, a plastic shoe tray is handy near the entrance of your home for wet or dirty boots. Store the boots and tray away in the off-season.

If you have children, create a designated place for backpacks so they are not thrown on the floor as soon as they come home, unless there are already hooks for them in the kids' bedrooms.

# Kitchen

You're more likely to cook if you have a clean kitchen to work in. Here are some tips to get the most out of your space and tools.

## Minimalist Cooking

Cooking at home is the best way to minimize your food budget and to ensure that you're eating healthy, wholesome food. And unless you're a master chef or an expert baker, you don't need as many items as you think. In fact, some of the best cooks use battered favorites or get creative with basics.

A basic kitchen requires a **stove top** and **refrigerator**. Many would say that an **oven** is required, but

I have lived in tiny European apartments without ovens and have survived. A **microwave oven** is despised by some, but indispensable for others. Personally, I wouldn't be able to last very long without one. Others will use it only occasionally to defrost things at the last minute, and it would not get enough use to justify the space it takes up. It's up to you.

As for basic gear, you need **a large pot**, **a small pot** and **a skillet**. The large pot can be used for stews, pasta, beans, etc, and the smaller pot is great for sauces, boiling small portions of vegetables, etc. Invest in hard-anodized aluminum pots and skillets and they will last you for decades.

A **paring knife** and a **chef's knife** will cover nearly all of your cutting needs. A **honing steel** will keep them usable. You also need a **cutting board** and a **vegetable peeler**. Sure you can use a knife instead of a peeler, but it's efficient, quick, and doesn't take much space.

If you are an occasional baker, you can get away with using two simple baking pans most of the time: a **9" by 13" cake-style pan** and **a French oven or casserole-style pan**. A **baking sheet** is handy to make homemade pizza, cookies, bread, and roasting vegetables. If you make meatloaves or other small casseroles, **a loaf pan** is great.

It's not essential, but a food processor is useful for cooking complex meals. Find a good one that you can use for chopping and grinding to juicing and pureeing.

Plastic or glass **reusable leftover containers** are always handy. Use masking tape to mark the name of what it contains on each container so that it's easily identifiable.

Think twice before buying items that have single uses. For example, cheese graters. Ask yourself if you grate cheese often enough to require one. Alternatively, you can use a multi-purpose item, such as a 4-in-1 **box grater** so that what you grate doesn't need to be limited to cheese.

Also look for creative substitutes. For example, you might not need a meat tenderizing hammer when a rubber mallet from your garage covered with a plastic bag can work just fine if you only need one once in a while.

Keep a well-stocked spice rack on hand. They're cheap and they'll add a kick to your meals.

## What to Avoid

Some of these items are essential to some, and absolutely useless to others. If you already own any of these, ask yourself when was the last time you've used the item and whether you can live without it.

**Stand Mixer**—Die hard bakers might find this to be worth the cost and space, but a simple whisk or electric beater is enough for most people. To cream butter and sugar, a food processor can work fine.

**Knife Sets**—They might look cool sitting on the counter, but most people don't need a full set of knives. A bread knife will probably be the only other knife you need if you eat a lot of bread.

**Bread Machine**—If you have a strong pair of arms and an oven, you can make excellent bread without one, and the bread won't always be the same square shape each time.

**Rice Cooker**—My Chinese friend would disagree, of course. If you eat rice once a week, a pot with a lid will do fine.

**Wok**—Again, unless you make Asian food all the time, you can use your large frying pan as a substitute.

**Pressure Cooker**—It can be useful, but do you need one?

**Pasta Maker**—Fresh pasta is readily available to buy and usually not too expensive.

**Toasted Sandwich Press**—Unless you eat sandwiches all the time, you can toast a sandwich in a frying pan, cooking one side at a time. It might taste even more delicious and crispier this way since the steam escapes as you cook, and not trapped.

**Bamboo Steamers**—If you don't steam pork buns often, you don't need them.

**Paella Pans**—Unless you're Spanish or obsessed with paella, a large frying pan is fine.

**Ice Cream Machine**—If you like to make homemade ice cream on occasion, there are many great machine-free recipes out there.

**Expensive Coffee Machine**—If you enjoy the ritual of going out to your local coffee shop to get your morning lattes, this might only gather dust.

**Other Single Purpose Appliances**—Juicers, milkshake machines, pop corn makers, deep fryers, hot dog warmers, popcorn makers, etc.

**Single Use Utensils**—Egg frying rings, lemon juicer, apple corer, strawberry dehuller, etc.

**Anything Ornamental**—Beautiful kitchen equipment can be decorative enough.

# Decluttering Tips

A clean, uncluttered kitchen may inspire you to cook more. Here are some tips for maintaining this space to make your life easier.

Remember that a kitchen is a place you cook in and eat in. Do you have items here that are unrelated to these two activities?

**1. Clear the Kitchen Counters**

If you only use the blender, toaster, or the food processor once or twice a week, store them out of sight. This also goes for junk mail lying around and bills that belong in the office. If the kitchen is the place you like to keep mail, use a designated basket or a wall mounted mail holder.

**2. Donate or Throw Things Out**

Make a habit of clearing out things you don't use. Donate those canned goods to local charities before they expire and throw out moldy food. Do your best to clean out the fridge weekly. Outdated dressing or sauces can be overlooked. Put expiring food at the forefront of shelves.

Purge old dishes, pots, pans and glassware. Donate them along with the things you never use.

### 3. Organize Cabinets, Drawers and Pantries

Organize your cabinets according to how you cook to make it easy. Keep dishes as close to the dishwasher as possible to make storing them easier.

If you have lots of pans, nest them, but avoid a deep stack because it'll make it hard to retrieve or return them. Put infrequently used ones in the back, or get rid of them altogether.

Maybe people have junk in their drawers, so sort through them often to make sure junk doesn't accumulate.

If you have a pantry, you're lucky. However, more space may mean more old food. Go through your food items, throw away the expired items and organize it by food type. Some lost items might even be rediscovered.

Store like with like. Put canned food together, snack foods, cereals, rice, pastas, etc.

### 4. Organize Your Spices

If you have a lot of spices, that's okay as long as you don't have three bottles of the same spice. A lazy Susan can take up too much counter space and it's not efficient in displaying your options when you have a lot of bottles. Invest in a good spice rack. It should have customizable labelling or display the spice bottle in a way that makes it easily identifiable.

### 5. Have One Place for Recipe Cards and Cookbooks

Are your recipe cards scattered all over the place? Store the loose recipes in a small binder, or keep index cards in a recipe box. Have one designated space for your cookbooks and recipes.

### 6. Keep Plastic Bags Contained and Accessible

Collect them in a small container with a hole so you can pull them out when you need them, or stuff them into an empty tissue box. Make them accessible under the sink.

The same rules apply if you have a very small kitchen. With even less space to work with, it forces you to pare down to the essentials even more.

## Living Room

The living room is one of the highly used places in your home. Don't put too much pressure on yourself to keep this space spotless. The key is to make the room livable.

A lot happens in a living room so it's more of a challenge to maintain, but start by identifying all the ways you use this space. Do you watch TV, read, nap, eat meals, exercise, play video games, etc, here? Know exactly what you do in this space and what you don't do, so that you can keep the things that are relevant to your activities, and remove the things that are not.

If you spend a lot of time in the living room, your stuff inevitably ends up accumulating on coffee tables and end tables. Encourage the members of your family to take what belongs to them to the rightful place, or to the trash.

If you have more than two remotes, label each one so you can find the one you need immediately. Have a designated spot for them, such as an end table or a remote holder that hangs from an arm of the couch.

If you have too many blankets and pillows, they can make the room look messy. If the blankets usually end up on the floor, use a basket without a lid so you can drop them in there with little effort.

If you have gaming consoles, you might end up with several controls and games. Wind up the cords of the controls when they're not in use and put them back on the shelf. Organize the games so that they're easily accessible. You might need a book end or two so that they stand upright instead of in messy stacks.

# Bathroom

Bathrooms can get crazy, especially when they are shared. To reduce clutter, buy basics such as toothpaste, shampoo and hand soap that everyone can use.

Bottles can overtake a bathroom. Finish, toss or give away half-used bottles before you start a new one. If you buy supersized bottles, pour them into small bottles for daily use and refill as needed. Keep the big bottles somewhere else, such as under a sink or in a closet.

If you love to take baths, keep a basket by the tub with all your favorite pampering essentials for easy access.

Create zones for each family member on the sink counter with decorative containers, and/or assign shelves. You can also assign a different color towel set to each person to avoid confusion.

Store hair accessories in a pretty basket or box. Look for one with divided sections. If you don't reach for them often, keep them out of sight.

Keep only the cosmetics you use. Many women love to collect makeup because the packaging is trendy or pretty, but they rarely reach for them. If you have cosmetics for evening only, keep them in a secondary place away from the counter. This also goes for the products you use on your travels.

If you really have a big collection and they are taking up a lot of room, keep them in a drawer with dividers. If your makeup must be on the counter, use baskets, or a small set of drawers to keep them sorted and at your fingertips. If you keep makeup in your purse, use a clear makeup bag to transfer them from purse to sink easily.

The space under the sink is usually big and you might want to maximize the space with removable shelves. Keep your cleaning products together in a tote bag and make sure they are out of reach from young children if you have them.

Keep toilet paper accessible. You might want to get a toilet paper holder to keep them upright to save space.

Maintain your first aid kit and label it well. Toss and replace expired items. Make sure everyone knows where it is and that it's easy to access.

If you've accumulated a lot of samples or travel-sized products, have a plan for them. Keep them in a ziplock bag for when you do travel, or for overnight guests. If you have a guest room, put some there.

If you need more space, install shelves on the vertical space over the toilet.

# Bedroom

Your bedroom is your sanctuary. It's a place to relax after a long day at work and a place to sleep. Make it a stress-free environment. Reconsider having your computer, television, ironing board, work papers, laundry, and any other extraneous or work-related items in the bedroom.

Limit items on your nightstand. An alarm clock, one photo and the book you are currently reading is enough, but not multiple books, especially if you are not reading them. Make sure your nightstand stays clean and clutter-free.

If you have an abundance of pillows on your bed, including decorative pillows, ask yourself if you really need them. How many pillows do you actually need to sleep? Do you put the decorative pillows on the floor at night when you go to sleep? They might be tripping hazards.

What's under your bed? The Black Hat style of Feng Shui says that it's best to keep the space under your bed clear so that your Qi energy will flow easily when you sleep. If you have, say, office supplies under your bed, you'll be thinking about work when you sleep, so be mindful of what you're keeping there. Put those things in their designated places.

Declutter the top of your dresser. Why is each item there and do they really belong there? If they don't have permanent homes, find one. Pamphlets can be filed or trashed, paper belongs on your desk, and broken items can either be repaired or tossed. Photos, a treasured figurine, and a jewelry box are lovely items to keep there so you'll be less tempted to clutter the space. If you have beautiful functional items, such as a perfume bottle or a jewelry tree, you can show them off there as well.

If you are really stuck when it comes to getting rid of the things in your bedroom, you need a new perspective. Get a box or bag, and collect your items. Take them outside and lay them out on the grass. Look at each item and ask if it is important to you. Now that it's taken out of your bedroom, does it really belong there? How do you feel about it? Does it support you? If not, toss it out. Only bring back the things that actually add value.

# Children's Rooms & Their Things

A children's room might be overrun with toys, games and stuffed animals. Tell your child that by getting rid of old toys, you'll give them room for new ones. The toys can be given to those who want them. Teach them the joy of giving.

Get a box and ask your child to tell you which toys or games they no longer want. If there are things they don't reach for anymore, but you want to keep them because you plan on having a second child, keep the things in a lidded container. Label it and store it.

If they have broken toys, either fix them or donate them. Make sure you do plan to fix them by a certain date or this task will slip through the cracks. Add this to the calendar with the deadline.

Revisit the toys every 2 to 3 months to see if there is anything that needs repairing.

If they have puzzles with missing pieces, try to find the pieces. If they're not found, toss it.

Stuffed animals can be everywhere, and if your child has too many, kindly ask family and friends to stop giving stuffed animals as presents and tell them that your child would prefer a different type of toy.

Label containers for easy cleanups. Use photos instead of words as labels if they are very young. This encourages them to be independent and clean after themselves.

If they are in school, they will probably come home with many graded assignments and it can be a challenge to contain them. Use a hanging holder in your filing cabinet for each child's work. At the end of the school year, go through the papers with your child to see which ones they can let go.

You may be too sentimental to throw out things such as clothes that no longer fit. Allow yourself to keep the most meaningful items. You might even make an art project out of it. For example, I once saw a great art project online that uses a baby shoe from each phase of a child's life. The shoes were framed inside a shadow box along with the age of the child written under each shoe.

If your child have a collection of school projects, such as science fair projects, take a picture of your child with the project. Then you are free to throw the project out if both of you agree. Keep the photo in the child's baby book or photo album.

They might also accumulate a lot of artwork. Give them a container or portfolio to store their art for the school year. If you have more than one child, clearly label the child's name and age, and store the container in a place that is accessible, such as the closet.

You can display their artwork throughout the house. Keep a photo frame or two in the hallway, for example, so that you can "curate" their work. Replace older art with the latest work. Store the older ones away neatly.

Work with your child to choose which ones they want to keep and which ones they are not as thrilled about so that they have control over the experience.

If the artwork gets to be too much, photograph them. Put the photos in a scrapbook or album. Create a separate album for each child.

# Teenager Bedrooms

If you have teenagers, let them know in a loving way that they are responsible for the cleanliness of their rooms. Explain that taking care of things will ensure that they last longer, and that they will be less stressed if they can find the things they need quickly.

When they do their own laundry on a regular schedule, they'll be able to wear their favorite clothes more often.

Food and dirty dishes will attract bugs and rodents and it's best if they eat in the kitchen.

If they keep sports equipment in their room, ask them if it'll be easier to keep them in the garage. If they need to access the equipment often, give them a container or box. If it's something they only use once a week, put it in a bag and hang it on a hook on the back of the door, in the closet or on a wall. If it's not used often, keep it in the back of the closet.

You can also agree to give them more privileges if they show responsibility and keep their rooms clean.

If they disagree, respect their choice as long as the food and dirty dishes are cared for. You can offer to help them if they are overwhelmed. Make a plan to do it on a day when you are both free.

Help them organize their school papers on their desk with a filing system and assign places for their textbooks. They might want to sell or donate old books or textbooks that they don't need anymore.

Their closets might also be full of items that they no longer wear or no longer fits them. Go through the questions from the "How to Recognize Clutter" chapter of this book to help them determine which things they can let go.

They are no longer children, so do not clean for them, especially when they have not given you permission to do so. Give them the freedom to make their own decisions. If you are actively keeping the rest of the house clean and clutter-free, they may be inspired enough to follow in your footsteps.

# Garage, Basement & Garden

**GARAGE**

Your car should be able to fit into your garage comfortably.

Pull your car into the garage and see how much space it takes up, including when you open the doors. Leave the doors open. This will help you determine how much stuff you need to get rid of.

Many people keep things in their garage for "just in case" events. If your ski equipment is taking up a lot of room and you only go skiing once every three years, consider selling the equipment and simply renting the next time you do go skiing.

If you have things like Christmas decorations, mark the boxes clearly.

Wall mounted organizers and hooks in the garage can be hung with brooms, mops, and bicycles. Take advantage of your vertical space.

If you have a lot of tools, use wall mounted tool racks for larger tools and sturdy storage bins for smaller stuff.

## BASEMENT

Don't store anything directly on the floor since flooding is a possibility. Instead of using cardboard boxes, use watertight plastic containers instead. Paper items such as newspapers and magazines will attract spiders so avoid storing them there, or throw them out all together. Paper items are fire hazards, so it's in the interest of your family's safety to get rid of them.

If you have pet food or birdseed, make sure they are in tightly closed containers to avoid attracting rodents.

## GARDENS

Assign an area for your garden stuff. This might mean your shed, the garage or the basement. Long handled tools, like the garden hose, can be wall mounted. Store fertilizers, seeds and the like in covered containers.

# Office

They say that a geniuses often keep a messy desk, but it's easier to create and get work done when your environment is organized. Thoughts flow better. Having what you need close at hand can only help you with mental clarity.

Your office, whether it's your real office at work, a room in your house, or simply a desk in the corner of your living room, would serve you best when it's clean and clutter-free.

Identify what you do in this space. Are you running a business? Writing a novel? Paying the bill? Writing letters? Researching on the computer? Snacking? Knitting? Hiding from the kids?

Now identify what you don't want to do in this room. Can you do these things elsewhere? If you like to snack, maybe you want to take the chocolate bars out of the drawer and back into the kitchen.

I once saw an exercise bike in the middle of a friend's office. I laughed because it symbolized that his work was really giving him a workout. That bike needed to go.

What do you need in the office in order to do the things you want to do? You'll most likely need a desk, a computer, a filing system and good lighting. Perhaps also a phone and a printer.

Clean the paper trail off your desk. Are you buried under paper, receipts, junk mail and food wrappers? Toss whatever you don't need.

Keep only the essentials on your desk, such as pens, a notepad, a stapler, or whatever else you reach for often. Keep the rest in a drawer. Limit personal items such as photos or decorative items to three or four. Tidy up when you are finished working each day.

If you're sharing a computer, create a separate folder for each family member so that documents don't get lost. If they argue over computer time, keep a calendar near the computer or share an online calendar to schedule computer times for each person.

If you read your mail here, set up a tray for incoming mail.

Are your papers really that valuable to you? Bills can be shredded as soon as they are paid. If you need to save them for a year or more, obtain at least one filing drawer. If you have a lot of paper, it might be necessary to have a two or three-drawer filing cabinet. It can be designated for family things as well, such as artwork, report cards, homework, etc.

When you open bills where you pay them, they are more likely to be paid. Why hold off on paying your bills until the last minute when you can do so immediately?

If you do need to pay bills later, place them on a desk tray or folder marked "BILLS TO PAY".

If you receive bills electronically, make a folder of the same name. When they are paid, move them to another folder called "BILLS PAID". It's faster to pay your bills online and you actually decrease the risk of fraud and identity theft by 10% or more.

You can also call up your bank and set up automatic payments so that you never forget. Go paperless whenever possible.

If you do need to write things down, instead of using sticky notes or loose paper, keep them in a notepad, planner or a notebook.

Do you have a huge to-do pile? Tackle them and make a realistic plan as to when you will complete them. If you have articles saved either online or printed for you to read, but you haven't gotten around to them, ask yourself if they are articles that really interest you or you feel obligated to read for whatever reason.

# Computer & Internet

**EMAIL**

Computers are supposed to make your life easier, not harder.

For many people, the computer is a personal environment. How do you feel when you use a computer? Do you feel drained and as if you'll never catch up with all the emails? Are you confused by all the files on your desktop? Make a conscious effort to develop better habits for the future.

Emails are like hits of caffeine. They give you energy but can drain you in the long run if you consume too much.

Don't answer emails at the most productive time of day. For some people, too many emails to start the day can distract them from the important tasks at hand.

Do you really need to be subscribed to all those newsletters? If not, unsubscribing is easy. If you want to keep them, they don't need to land in your inbox. By creating a separate folder, and filtering the emails, they'll appear in that folder so you can read them when you have the time.

Do you really need to archive your messages? You might want to go back and purge the emails every few months. It's good practice to delete emails immediately after you read them, especially those that don't require an action. If you're unsure whether to delete the email, you can always file them.

Filing your emails in categories such as "Receipts", "Bills to Pay", "Travel Confirmations", "Photos", and so on, will make it easier to go back and find the email you're looking for.

Folders can be a great way to organize email, but be aware if you are using them to hide things that you don't want to see. Face each email head on. Either tackle them, make a plan to tackle them at a designated time, or delete them.

If you get too many emails from friends or family, delete the ones that are not important. Do you really need to respond to all of them?

Go through your email contacts and delete the people you are no longer in contact with. You may also find it beneficial to sort the contacts by groups such as "family", "friends", "business", etc.

If your business requires you to be accessible by email 24/7, take a look at how much of your emails actually require your immediate action. When you don't need to respond right away, you don't have to.

If you're the type who needs to reply right away because otherwise you'd forget, you can flag those emails, or create a "To Reply" folder to put them in. Life is for living. Don't let emails suck up your time.

If others ask you why you're not responding to their emails as fast as you used to, kindly explain that you're taking it easy with your technology. Let them know your new relationship with email and how often you're using it now. This might give them the hint to ease off on emailing you all the time and communicate with you in other ways. After all, it's more personal—and fun—to exchange news face to face.

For other email-happy friends, you might have to let them know in a gentle way that you don't have time for excess emails and emailing. Some people can happily waste time emailing at work as a distraction, but you don't need to participate if you have better things to do.

Gain control of your time by setting a specific time during your day when emailing is convenient for you. If you limit your time to, say, thirty minutes or an hour of emailing per day, you can give your full attention to the emails that deserve it. This means that when you do respond, you're in the headspace to do so in a way that's thoughtful, concise and adds value to the receiver.

When you email someone else, ask yourself the same thing: will your email add value to someone else's life?

## BROWSER

Go through the bookmarks you've saved on your browser. Which ones are you no longer visiting? Delete them.

Identify subjects and organize the bookmarks. For example, if you visit a lot of cooking sites, group them together. It will save you time when you're looking for the links.

## SOCIAL NETWORKS

Do you even use them, or do you have phantom profiles floating around different sites? Delete the accounts you don't use, or those that are not serving your life in a positive way.

It might feel as if everyone is online these days, but you don't need to cave into the pressure of a 2-D representation of your life if that doesn't appeal to you. There are better things to do with your time!

## DESKTOP

Is your desktop covered with folders and documents? Open each one up and ask yourself if you really need the information, or if you can delete it.

Group like with like. If you have many photos for example, put them in the same photo file under different sub files for events, people, and so on.

If you don't need to access certain files on a regular basis, you can move them to a hard drive or email them to yourself to free up your computer space.

**INTERNET**

Do you need internet on your cell phone? Do you even need it at home? Some people claim that they can't live without 24/7 internet access, but they probably haven't given it a fair shot.

If you limit your internet access, you won't be checking your emails every few minutes, Googling random things, and getting distracted by funny Youtube videos when you should be working.

Try limiting your internet time, perhaps to only an hour a day. This might be torture at first, but eventually you might find that you need the internet less than you think.

Every time you get the urge to Google something, write it down to remind yourself to do it later. This might turn into a list. When you do get access to the internet, you can refer to this list. You may even wonder why you ever wanted to waste your time searching some of these subjects to begin with.

If having the internet at home is an absolute must, reconsider internet access on your mobile. At the very least, hide the email app on your phone so you don't feel the compulsion to check every new email that comes your way.

## Technology

If you have outdated computers, phones, stereos, and other technology lying around at home, why are you keeping them? Unless you love the item (many vintage cameras, for example, are beautiful), feel free to let them go. Ask your local tech store how you can recycle or dispose your old devices safely. Some stores buy used phones and computers, even though the price offered might be a small fraction of its original value. You can also donate certain items to your local charity shop.

For the items you want to keep, care for them. Don't store cameras and other gadgets under direct sunlight, near a heater or in a car parked under the sun. This also goes for very cold or humid places.

Store them in their cases when not in use to protect them from dust, liquid, accidental falls, etc.

If you have a lot of owner manuals, tear out the foreign language sections so that they're not so bloated. Staple the sales receipt and warranty on the inside covers. Keep the manuals together in a binder with plastic page protectors, or file them in your filing cabinet.

Don't leave chargers plugged into outlets when not in use. They will suck up energy.

## Closets

It's easier to get dressed in the morning when you can quickly find the clothes you need and they are wrinkle-free.

Envision how you want your closet to look. Do you want your clothes sorted by type or by color? Do you want more hooks for your belts and accessories? Do you need more hangers or maybe you have too many?

Take inventory of what you own. By noticing what you already have, you'll be less tempted to buy similar items when you are shopping.

Get rid of sentimental clothes—clothes that you think are going to make a comeback or will fit if you could only lose ten pounds.

Ask yourself:

**Have I worn this in the last year?**

**Does this go with anything?**

**Am I waiting to lose/gain weight to fit back into it?**

**Am I only keeping this because it's expensive?**

Donate the clothes that no longer fit you. Same with the items you rarely wear because they are uncomfortable.

Remove the clothes that are damaged. Either repair them yourself, take them in to a shop, or throw them away.

Strive to fill your closet to no more than 75% capacity. This will make it easier to retrieve and rehang items.

If you're having a really hard time knowing what to give away, try this trick: Rehang all your items so that the hooks face you. When you take out an item to wear, hang them back the regular way with the hanger facing the wall. After a month, you'll be able to see which pieces you've left untouched.

Store belts and ties in a way where you can remove one and return it without disturbing the others. One way is to fold them up in a way that won't wrinkle them. There are also special hangers for ties, belts and accessories that will save you space.

If you keep many of your clothes in drawers, rolling clothes up can help you save space and make them easier to grab. Match socks up and pull down one sock opening over both socks so they're easier to grab by the pair.

Make sure the storage space for your seasonal or infrequently used items is clean, dry and airy with no direct sunlight. Almost everything should be folded and put into covered containers or a cedar chest if you have one. This will protect your things from dust, insects and rodents.

Unless you travel frequently, suitcases can be used to store seasonal clothes, linen and even holiday decorations. Label the address tags with the content and owner's name. Otherwise, you can keep them in one side of the closet or in another storage space.

Avoid using mothballs in any of your storage. While they do reel moths, they're toxic to breathe. Use cedar blocks or chips instead.

If you have attractive vintage suitcases, stacking two or three of them together can make a great bedside table.

If you have children, at least one of them will have hand-me-downs. Ask them whether they even like the items. If not, donate them.

Other than donating your clothes, you can sell them if they are expensive. You can do this online, at consignment stores, or hold a garage sale. You can also organize a clothing swap with your friends. Get together one evening with your friends at someone's place and bring what you don't want to keep. Check out the other items that are up for grabs. Just be careful not to come back with more things you won't wear!

Keep the shoes you wear frequently near the front door. The others you can keep in your closet. You can use the classic trick of keeping the shoes in their boxes and sticking a photo of the shoes in front of the box.

**LINEN CLOSETS**

Do you know what your linens are for? Do they match? Make sure you don't have too many linen sets. Three is the maximum for any given bed: one for the bed, one for the laundry and one in the closet. This goes for towels as well.

Separate items by type: pillowcases, bath towels, hand towels, linen for master bedroom, kid's bed, etc. If possible, label the shelf. Perhaps you can add extra shelves or dividers to make things easier to grab. If you have to pull out a towel underneath a stack of hand towels and thick robes, you'll have an even harder time of putting them back properly. This is how messes are created, so it's easier if you make items accessible.

Don't keep vacuum cleaners, shoes, sports equipment or anything else that gathers dust in this closet.

## Minimalist Wardrobe

While you don't need a lot of money to look good, do invest in some quality pieces. They will last you in the long run.

Some people will say that a minimalist wardrobe should consist of a number of items. Limiting yourself to 10 or 15 pieces is not practical for everyone. However, do take note of the 10 pieces you do wear the most often by putting them to one side of your closet. You'll see how well certain pieces can serve you. This will illuminate what you really wear, and it'll help you pack light for your next vacation.

Know what kind of style you like or want to adopt. Are you wearing pieces that you already love and wear all the time? Do you dress a certain way because you have to (example, for an office job)? Are you too afraid to branch out and try new styles?

If you've realized that you don't wear many of the pieces in your closet and have gotten rid of them, here are some tips for when you go shopping for new clothes:

• Buy versatile pieces that you can mix and match together. Most of the items in your wardrobe should go with each other. It's best to buy items that are not overly formal or too casual so you can dress up or down. For example, a top can be worn to the grocery store or to a dinner party with the addition of jewelry or a scarf. A pencil skirt that can be worn at the office or for after hours. A classic coat can be thrown on for your daily school runs or on a night out.

• Choose classic styles and silhouettes that flatter your body. This might mean straight-legged pants, A-line or pencil skirts, and classic shift dresses. Or it might not. Some people look great in skinny jeans and other people don't. If you're not sure what's flattering, you might need to try things on. Things that look just okay on the rack might look amazing on you, or vice versa. You never know unless you try it on.

- Even when something looks good on you, do you *feel* good in it? Are you comfortable moving around and sitting down? Would you be proud to be photographed with it on?

- Neutral and well-fitted basics for pants, skirts and suits will serve as a base for your wardrobe.

- Choose accent colors that compliment your skin tone. You know which shades look good on you and which ones are not so flattering. Ask for a second opinion from a friend if you're unsure.

- Avoid buying clothes that you know you will hardly wear. If it's a piece that's on-trend that might be out in a few months, skip it or buy a less expensive version of the outfit.

- Make sure everything fits—now. If you have minor weight fluctuations, choose fabrics with a bit of stretch.

- Choose accessories that will go with your wardrobe. Bags and shoes in neutrals will get more use and you won't need them in multiple colors to match. If you really love those neon orange pumps, life is short so why not? Just be aware of how much you will reach for them.

- Don't shop with sales goggles on. It's tempting to buy loads of pretty pieces or vintage when they're cheap, but be honest with yourself as to whether you can see yourself wearing the pieces you're interested in on a regular basis. Plus, buying things on sale don't save you money.

- Dress in layers. Cardigans will add more versatility than season-specific clothes.

# Minimalist Car

**Go Car-Free**

Ask yourself: do you need a car? This is doable for many people living in the center of a city. If you're unsure, you can start small and test out what car-free living feels like by leaving your car in your garage for a week and running your errands by foot, bike or public transit.

Car ownership can be costly and you're spending more time sitting instead of walking more or biking in the fresh air. You'll also truly experience your city or town if you walk or bike. It allows you to slow down and observe your surroundings, and interact with local neighbors and business owners.

**Go Car-Lite**

However, if you feel a car is necessary for you and your family, don't feel guilty. If a car is giving value to your life by saving you time and making your life easier, that's a good thing. Simply reconsider how much you're depending on your car and whether you can use it less often.

Consider getting rid of any extra cars. If your family can get by with one or two cars, you don't need three. What about other vehicles such as motorcycles and scooters?

### Minimalist Car

A car's function is to get you from point A to point B. It's not a moving closet. Blankets, first aid kits, flashlights, car scraper (when it's winter), Help signs, and other emergency items are appropriate. Trash, broken tools, alcohol and random junk are not.

If there's a lot of stuff in your car, grab some boxes and take everything out—even the spare change and napkins. If there are things you never use, and they are not for emergencies, ask yourself if they are giving you value by staying.

Ask:

**When did I use this last?**

**Why is this in my car?**

**Is this need related to my car? Why?**

**If I don't put this back in my car, what might be the consequences?**

This might be time consuming, but it'll result in a less cluttered car that you'll feel good to drive in.

## Mail

Catalogs, junk mail, bills, invitations and magazines can clog your mailbox on a daily basis. When you can, unsubscribe from the junk list. Sometimes a request to your building concierge or placing a small sign on your mailbox saying "No Junk Mail Please" will reduce unnecessary mail.

Do the same with your regular mail. Opt out of special credit card offers, charitable donation requests and the like if you don't want them.

If you subscribe to magazines, ask yourself if they are publications you actually read. Are you genuinely excited to receive them or do you barely glance at them once you do? Are you reading out of a sense of obligation, such as the need to feel smarter or the need to be prettier?

Certain magazines can make us feel inferior. Women's magazines send out the message that women must live up to an ideal. It's liberating then to simply stop reading.

Another example is travel magazines. If you read them because you long to go on faraway adventures, but you feel bad because your life is so busy that you can't travel as often as you like, you can give yourself permission to stop reading. After all, when you do plan your next vacation, travel information is always available.

Magazines are heavy and take up a lot of room. Don't forget that magazines are free to read at your local library. Many magazines also offer digital editions these days.

If you subscribe to newspapers and keep them, remember that they can be fire hazards so it's best to recycle them after you read them. If you want to keep certain articles, keep them in a scrapbook.

You can remove yourself from catalog lists or magazine subscriptions by calling their customer service number. Give them your customer code or the ID on your address label and politely ask them to remove you.

When you recycle the catalogs and magazines, be sure to rip your name and address label off before you do.

With bills, it's ideal to open and throw away the envelope as soon as it arrives, as inserting it back into the envelope is a waste of energy. Pay it right away, or put it in your "To Pay" folder.

Keep only the invites and events you want to attend, unless you want to call in regrets, which is best to do right away if you're forgetful.

## Collections

Even if you don't consider yourself a collector of anything in particular, we all have collections. Whether it's books, shoes, and magazines, we can accumulate many things without even realizing it. This section will provide some tips on how to manage, minimize or stop some of the more common collections.

## Automatic Collections

Sometimes collections are unintentional. Hobby-related items, or gifts that friends and family give you related to a theme can snowball out of control. They might have showered you with gifts to contribute to the collection because these gifts require little creativity while being a safe bet.

To determine whether you want to keep this collection or not, ask yourself:

**Does this collection make me happy?**

**Do I enjoy looking at it?**

**Does it serve a practical purpose in my home?**

**Does it show off my interests and personality?**

**Does it relax me?**

**Am I pursuing it out of habit?**

**Do I want to continue collecting?**

If you realize that you don't want to continue collecting, first give yourself permission to stop. The collection might be expensive to pursue or to maintain, it might take up a lot of space, and/or is giving you anxiety.

Kindly ask your family members to stop contributing to the collection. Simply explain that you've adopted a more minimalistic way of living if you want to give a reason.

If your collection is inherited, consider whether you want to hand it down to your children one day. Would they even want them, or would it cost them time/money/energy to do so?

Find a good home for your collection if you feel guilty for letting it go. Give them to people who would appreciate it. Take a picture of yourself with the entire collection if it's something you want to remember.

Ask family members if they want certain items. If you plan on passing your collection on to your kids, understand that they might not want them, even if the items are expensive. If your children are grown, ask them for honest feedback as to whether they want it or not.

# Sentimental Objects and Gifts

It's not easy to throw away objects and gifts from close friends and family, especially those who have passed on.

Make the distinction that when you toss stuff out, it doesn't mean tossing the person away. Sometimes it can feel like it because we've attached meaning and a story to the object.

If your grandmother gave you a lamp before she passed away, but you personally hate the lamp, what would she care what you do with it now that she's in the afterlife? She's not going to be offended.

To help you let go, you can always take a picture of the object, put it in a scrapbook and write down the memory you get from it. That way, you can transfer the memory from the object to your scrapbook.

## Photos

Photos can be a great way to bring back happy memories. Since we are in the digital age, we've become more snap-happy, so we are taking and storing more photos than ever.

If you keep a lot of photos, ask yourself why. Are they to honor memories or to relive the past? Are you afraid of throwing away or deleting a photo because you don't want to lose the memory?

Being aware of why would help you decide what you can keep or let go.

So which photos should you keep? The simple answer is the ones you really love—the ones that make you feel happy and grateful for the experience.

Go through the photos one at a time. Keep the ones that jump out at you. Feel free to get rid of hum drum photos, duplicates, and unflattering photos.

Note if any photos conjure up painful feelings. For example, if you keep pictures of your ex-lovers but feel pain when you look at them, why keep them around? Are you keeping them because you long for those moments and you don't believe you'll experience the same happiness again? Letting go of the past, especially the painful moments, allows you to open your present life to new experiences.

Many people get so caught up in taking pictures on their vacations that they don't take the time to fully enjoy the moment and really take in their surroundings. While it's not a crime to take photos on vacations, it's best to have a balance so that you're not living life from behind a camera lens.

Digital cameras and smartphones allow you to take hundreds of photos in a single outing. A vacation can even result in thousands of photos. It's good practice to go through all your photos at the end of each day. Delete the blurry or unflattering photos right away, as well as duplicates and photos you aren't fond of.

At home, sort them in categories that make sense, whether it's by year, event, or person. This goes for digital and hard copy photos.

For hardcopy photos, you can make photo albums, scrap books or display them in frames.

For digital photos, you can use programs like Picasa and iPhoto to organize photos, edit them, make digital albums, or even create photo books that you can print on demand.

You can also display digital photos in a digital photo frame so you have a constant slideshow and a variety of photos on display so you won't have to print them.

## Cards & Letters

Do you keep all the birthday cards, invitations, postcards and letters that you receive? They are lovely, especially in the digital age, but you don't need to feel obligated to keep all of them.

Cards and letters that communicate a thought or a feeling can be let go after you receive them. For example, if you receive a card wishing you a happy birthday, you've acknowledged that a friend has conveyed their well-wishes for you. You're not a bad person if you want to let go of the card. You can't hold on to every thought and feeling, otherwise you'd be drowning in them.

This also applies for ecards and emails. After expressing your thanks, feel free to hit the delete button.

Of course if you receive well thought out handwritten letters and cards, and you want to look back on them in the future, do so. Keep the ones you cherish and would read again.

## Music

It's easy to accumulate a lot of music in the digital age. With a click of a button, you can download whatever song you want.

If you still keep CDs and other physical music albums, you can digitize the contents to lighten up your collection.

It's a little more difficult to let go of music because it's an artform that can be enjoyed repeatedly, as opposed to books that can be read once or twice. You might feel the need to keep outdated music around just in case you ever get in the mood to listen to it again. However, this might mean keeping hundreds or thousands of outdated songs around that you rarely listen to. The choices may overwhelm you and make it more difficult to find the songs you actually do want to listen to. If an old song does strike your fancy, music streaming has made it easy to find any song online with a click of a button.

Go through each song in your collection. Ask yourself if you would buy this music and listen to it in the present. The first answer is usually the right answer. If you're still in doubt, play the song and ask yourself how it makes you feel. Do you like that feeling?

Consider letting go of songs or albums that you haven't listened to in the last six months. This is easy to do because programs like iTunes or your music player can tell you when you've played the song last.

By cleaning out your collection, you'll end up with good music that you'll actually listen to on a regular basis.

## Digital Decluttering

Even though digital books, photos, songs or documents don't weigh as much, you still have to be careful of keeping digital clutter. Free ebook titles are available every day, and many people don't think twice about downloading them just because they are free. Sometimes they'll end up with hundreds of books on their Kindles that they'll never read, just taking up space and making it difficult to find the books they do want.

If you haven't opened, played or used a digital file in the last six months, consider getting rid of it. Purge your collection twice a year.

# People

Perhaps you manage your contacts the old fashion way, through address books and Rolodexes. Make sure your list is updated regularly because people do move or change numbers.

You can also store contacts on your computer, but make sure to back it up. You can sync your smartphone contacts with the contacts on your email list so you won't lose your database if you lose you phone. Maintaining a digital contact list, especially one on your phone, is great, because it gives you each person's information at your fingertips. When someone has a birthday coming, there are apps to remind you or sync the date to your calendar so you'll never forget someone's birthday again.

If you have stacks of business cards, consider inputting the information from the contacts you need on your list so you can get rid of the cards. Alternatively you can use a business card holder. You can also manage a digital database of cards by using business card apps where you can scan the card with the phone's camera and save it as a digital file.

**RELATIONSHIPS**

As you go through your contact list, are you finding people that you haven't contacted for a while, and don't plan on contacting again? Don't feel bad if you want to remove them from your database—or your life.

Sometimes we form relationships out of convenience, such as with coworkers, classmates or even lovers. It can be easier to stay in those relationships because new friendships are more of a challenge to start. While it may require effort to release the old friends who are no longer adding much value to your life, anything worthwhile requires a bit of effort.

Are you holding on to toxic or energy-draining friends simply because you've known them since middle school? Are you staying with a lover simply because you're not sure that you can do better? Are you holding on to someone who doesn't deserve a place in your life?

If a person is not supportive of you, takes more than he or she gives, and prevents us from growing and experiencing new things, take a deeper look at your relationship. Victims can be victimizers. They keep us from reaching our true potential. They carve a place in our lives, thus our identities. Friends who are constantly playing the victim, complaining and subsequently dragging you down with them don't add value to your life.

However, keep in mind that nobody is perfect. We all complain or get down on the dumps once in a while. People can change, or simply need a wake up call to know that how they are behaving is affecting you in a negative way.

See if the relationship is salvageable. Talk to them in a loving way as to what needs to change for the relationship to work. Tell them what you need, such as support, less gossiping, or no more put-downs.

Then ask them what they'd like to change in the relationship and how you can improve and add more value to their lives as well. Listen carefully to their response. You can tell a lot about a person by how they react.

If they blame you for everything and refuse to take responsibility, you can make your own decision as to whether you want to continue this relationship or not.

This can be incredibly difficult especially if it is a family member, lover or a long-time friend. But if they are mostly draining your time, self-esteem and energy, don't feel guilty about limiting your time with them, or cutting them from your life all together.

You're also doing them a favor because you are giving them an opportunity to change and grow, if they are open to it. If they don't, don't press the issue. They'll simply think you're judging them when they haven't asked for your critiques to begin with.

When you stop accepting the people who don't deserve a spot in your life, you make room for people who do. The people closest to you should be those who love you, encourage you and add value to your life.

What you don't want to do is point fingers and blame them. If they are not getting the message that you want to be treated with respect, your actions speak louder than words: walk away. Usually there's no need to tell people you've decided to let them go. Usually they will drift away naturally.

You don't win if you stay in a friendship or relationship where you are suffering simply out of guilt or obligation. In fact you'll grow resentment towards them. You can't change people, but if you don't want to be around them, you can put space between you so you have room to breathe and grow.

If you're having a hard time determining whether someone has a place in your life, sit down at a desk and look at a photo of them. Ask yourself whether they really add positivity to your life, or unnecessary weight. Your initial feeling is usually the right one.

As you grow in a positive way, you'll attract like-minded people. That's the law of attraction: like attracts like. Energetically, the people you once had things in common with might not be on your level anymore and it's only natural that you grow apart.

You owe it to yourself to be happy. Be in control of your own life. Do the things you are passionate about and surround yourself with new, empowering relationships.

Relationships also goes both ways. Are you adding value to other people's lives? Are you dumping your frustrations on others? Are you taking more than you're giving? Are you truly interested in the other person, or what they can do for you? Do you support your loved ones or criticize their choices? Do you spend quality time with them or only when it's convenient for you?

Both people must do their part for the relationship to continue and grow. That's what makes it a partnership. Both must contribute equally.

## Other People's Clutter

You might own clutter that doesn't even belong to you. They could be things belonging to a former roommate, a former flame, or things left by friends and family that they haven't gotten around to picking them up.

Contact the owner to collect the item. If it's someone who is not giving you a firm date and time to come over, give them a deadline. Explain that you're making space in your home and arrange a time for them to pick it up that's convenient for the both of you.

If you haven't seen the person in a long time and haven't heard from them, feel free to dispose of the item.

## Minimalist Checklist

It's a good idea to question your possessions on a regular basis. Understand that things can be replaced. Let go of the things that no longer serve you. Don't forget to ask:

**Does it have long term value?**

**Do I really need this?**

**When was the last time I used this?**

**Could someone else use this more than me?**

## Maintain Your Space

You'll need discipline if you don't want to go back to the mess where you started. Of course life is messy and imperfect, but it can be manageable. All you need is a system, a plan for your stuff.

For example, if you're still subscribed to a few magazines because you love reading them, designate a place for unread magazines so you know where you can find them when you have the time to read them. If toys are always scattered in the living room, have a bin close by and teach your children to help you clean up. Get them to do it themselves if they are old enough.

Make sure your things are reachable. If you're not storing your pots away because you need to use them all the time, it's better to hang them in sight, or leave the ones you use on the stove.

Periodically weed out more clutter—at least once a year. Just because your things are neatly stored in boxes and bins, it doesn't mean they are adding value to your life.

Clearly label all the boxes and bins for long-term storage (ex. winter clothes, sports equipment, etc). This way you won't be wondering where they are when you need them.

Make your flat surfaces too beautiful for clutter. Keep it clean and put out fresh flowers if you like them.

Tidy up after yourself whenever you use a space.

# Conclusion

There's something absolutely liberating about owning less and having less options. It costs less, it requires less time and energy to maintain, and it welcomes freedom and calm in our hectic daily life.

With clutter out of the way, we invite the greater opportunity to pursue our true passions and spend our precious time on the things we enjoy with the people we love.

As you practice the art of minimalist living, you'll want to own less. In our consumeristic society, this might be even more valuable than owning less.

Growth is ongoing so continue to purge your superfluous possessions. Choose long-lasting fulfillment over temporary fixes. It's never too late. Live in the moment. You have the space and energy to do that now. Spend time with the people you love. Spend time in solitude in a bare room, enjoying your own company. Whatever you do, pursue a life with all your heart.

*– Elizabeth N. Doyd*

# About the Author

Elizabeth N. Doyd is the author of the bestselling books *Write Him Off: Journal Prompts to Heal Your Broken Heart in 30 Days*, and *Gratitude Journal: 52 Writing Prompts to Celebrate Your Wonderful Life*. She also works as a relationship expert and spiritual counselor, having studied Kabbalah, Buddhism, hypnotherapy, astrology and Reiki.

Originally from Montana, Elizabeth has traveled around the world and currently lives in The Hague, Netherlands, with her husband, son and two Scottish terriers. Her highly practical self-help books are for those looking for guidance and healing in love, wealth and self-worth, and how to live each day with love, joy and purpose.

www.ingramcontent.com/pod-product-compliance
Lightning Source LLC
Chambersburg PA
CBHW031453040426
42444CB00007B/1080